Nearly Fifty

a collection of essays

PALOMA A. CAPANNA

PAGE PUBLISHING, INC.
New York, NY

First originally published by Page Publishing, Inc. 2018

ISBN 978-1-64214-568-7 (Paperback)
ISBN 978-1-64298-381-4 (Hardcover)
ISBN 978-1-64214-569-4 (Digital)

Printed in the United States of America

Atop the Mountain

There was a time I would not have lit a fire, if there wasn't a man at home to tend to it. That worry wore off long ago, out of need.

Tonight, it was the widespread September hatching of flies that had me do it. A disgusting and unexpected moment on a day a friend committed suicide. The air was rife with gnatty-buggy things, seeming to be rising up out of the ground. At the same time, they seemed to be dropping out of the sky, raining out of the trees, at the edge of the woods.

The fire, though smoking, wasn't turning fast enough into heat-filled smoke. The bugs were undeterred, some dropping with a tap onto the metal firebox, before hitting the ground and walking away.

I threw the dog into the trailer. He'd been earlier to the vet and was sufficiently logy to make an easy target.

As the fire grew, the low cloud ceiling broke, and blessedly, a breeze came through.

It was going to be a good fire and a good sunset. The bank of clouds shifted south. There was a break of blue. Up north, Raphaelesque clouds promised to reflect pinks and August gold.

"Hoonayo, hoonayo, ho nay ap ea. Hoonay ap ea."

I sang a made-up tune of syllables without any meaning beyond my intention to summon my ancestors to meet Bill as he ascended. It's unclear to me how all of this is supposed to work. Just four months ago, I had lost a dear friend, Ed, to suicide. Since then, work had been so bloody nuts that it had forcibly carried me along. All that broke, only yesterday, as I sat at my desk, staring at the condolences card I bought, right away, but hadn't sent to Ed's parents, there being no funeral. This time, people would come together, anyway. Bill was a public official. Ed, a mere boy.

What is there to say or do?

A twenty-something-year-old allegedly put a gun to his head and pulled the trigger. A fifty-nine-year-old put a gun to his head and pulled the trigger. Both were upper-middle class Caucasian American males. Both successful by any work-standard metric. Both smiled and laughed and were sociable. Yet both have died in a matter considered sinful and illegal.

A gunshot goes off in the distance. Out here, in this rural area of this open farm countryside, a regular enough occurrence. Hell, I shoot .22 and .308 and not often enough for my preference. Coyotes routinely sing down in what we dubbed "Coyote Holler," and next year we'll add livestock to our new farm. My permit application is overdue. I support the Second Amendment.

Two male turkeys are on parade, practicing, presumably, since I'm the only female for about a mile and a half. I wouldn't mind one for a free Sunday dinner. It's still too early, though, to get any tags.

Betty Friedan was so busy putting women in boardrooms that she forgot to notice an entire class of tougher-than-a-feminist: the farm wife.

Truthfully, I can't claim to be that yet, on either of two fronts. I'm only just getting started on this hundred-acre farm and I'm nobody's wife.

In between the thoughts, the words, the song, the dog, there is movement. Could be anything. I add wood to the fire. I feed the dog his dinner. I grab Ayn Rand's *Atlas Shrugged* that I bought a month ago at a church flea. It's my third or fourth copy, others lost to unreturned loans, ex-husbands, and boxes that seemed to disappear every time I managed to move. This paperback copy is essentially new, unopened, and saying, "Finally? Will you finally have time to read me the way you read *The Fountainhead* and fell in love with yourself through the mirror of Roark?"

And it's right, this book. This book resting on the left arm of this barn-found rattan chair. I'm now nearly fifty, and the change is starting at last.

Several years of perimenopause later, I've started the sweats from the crown of my head throughout the whole of me. It explains all these fires that I've been burning in the summer of the greatest drought of my life. Fire early morning "to make the coffee." Fire afternoon "to clear out the skunk wood." Fire in the evening "to summon up the coyotes." All the time, encouraging sweat.

If I could just bring myself to be doing yoga, in the way I have done it for years. But it's an odd sense of fatigue that has invaded my bones. A new kind of tired that is a betrayal of the body I've known and once loved. No more the fighting with it of these past several years, but now a disappointment I can't explain. It causes me to sit when really I have more to do in this waning light.

The half-moon has risen. Bill's wife soon faces her first night alone in decades. What must be the silence of it all, after being married to a man in the spotlight? After media questions (now turned to you) and calls to your children with the news?

Two months ago, how nearly I lost my own man—the man I call a "husband," who is not. The foreshadowing of an afternoon nap, not ever taken by a man raised up on a farm. The look upon his face as he laid his head against my chest, when I sat on the bed, somehow bracing, recognizing that it was a potential sign. And then *the* look. And then the words, "I think I need to go to the doctor."

I don't know what to do with the fact of people dying and in this way. Numbers four and five of the suicides among people I've known.

And my man? Only fifty-three and they call his specific type of heart attack "the widow maker" from which only one in three survives.

Kevin confessed that it started the day before. That when it started, he left the farm and drove two hours to get back to me.

I was working at the time, at our current, suburban home.

We're still building the house, here at the farm.

So how's that, Gloria and Ruth? Me at a computer while the truest love I had not dared to imagine might have died all alone atop this mountain.

Thanks be to God; Kevin didn't die that afternoon.

At least I can be confident that we won't die by our own hands.

The fire, long ago, chased away all of the bugs. The half-moon has risen high. Right now, I simply wait. Wait for the stars. Count on the darkness of a cloudless sky. Hope when Sleep comes that She will gently come.

Anonymous

People don't believe that I saw a wolf. They say there are no wolves in New York. They say it was a coyote. I say and show a photograph from the seven I shot, and they say they need to see a better photograph.

Is it because I was a woman alone with a camera and not a rifle?

He was breathtaking. Huge and majestic. I spotted him at about 250 yards on the field side of a border of wildflowers and scrub afore the pine trees along the southern boundary of the farm.

At first thought: *a deer.* Then: *wolf.* Then: *coyote.* Then: *wolf— definitely wolf.* The unmistakable thickness of fur, the white fur rim inside his ears. Thoughtful eyes, strong neck, white bib, broad chest, canine muzzle. The size at about 120 pounds.

How does one identify anything?

Look at any politician in Albany; you will recognize the face of corruption.

I am amazed, more stunned today than yesterday, at the number of lawsuits, judgments, and investigations concerning Bill now splayed all over the press. One day after his death. The dollars involved aren't small.

How does one avoid corruption in 2016?

7

It's gotten too expensive to live. With minimum wage at $15/hour, an ice cream cone approaches $5, if it's made on site. Teenagers, barely out of their parents' houses, have driven up the cost of goods through the doubling of the minimum wage. Have other wages and salaries gone up 50%? No. And so the equation actually represses the majority of working men and women for the benefit of a fraction of the workforce.

I take a photograph of our dog, looking longingly at about sixteen turkeys strutting across the lower, east field. On Facebook, more friends like that photo in fifteen minutes than all four likes combined for my shot of my wolf.

My wolf. Now there's a thought. One long encounter and I've claimed him?

I got off three frames before he saw me. His attention was elsewhere, as I turned and I saw him. But then he turned and looked at me. I wasn't the scent that had been filling his nostrils—what was I?

One Mississippi. Two Mississippi. *You're going to want to know how long this was so you can tell it with accuracy.*

And then he approached. Came directly toward me, covering about one-third of the distance.

And I thought: *I can't win this, if it's that moment.*

I've said for decades, when my time comes, I'm going to go off into the woods and be taken by a bear. I believe this to be true. I can see me, gray haired and of wild woman beauty, and ready as the swipe rips open my cheek, catches my hair.

He stopped. He studied me. I raised my camera, taking three more frames.

It's true. The Canon 60D, yes, but the lens only 24-105 and not suited for long-distance wildlife photography. He is a bit grainy on the enlargement, and yet he is so unmistakably a wolf.

I put the camera slowly down. I've spent much of my free time behind that lens. This wolf? I wanted to see him, wanted to know him, wanted to feel him if his intention became to further approach.

One moment more... But he flipped his nose upward, turned tail, and trotted back to the Canada Goldenrod along the far edge. And then he turned and repositioned until our gaze was locked upon each other.

Some while later, he went a few paces to his left, turned left through those Goldenrods, passed between two pine trees, and disappeared from sight.

I walked forward. Possessed. As the women of fable are wont to do. Closed half of the distance between where he had disappeared and I had once stood. Walked away from the woman I had been and toward the woman I wanted to become.

Then, I spoke to him. Introduced myself by my name, "Paloma," and I spoke to him some words to confirm and to validate our friendship. I told him that a day might come that each could need the other. That I would keep him a secret and ward off hunters from this site.

And then, shortly, I saw them rising and coming toward me: my man and our Redbone, pulling hard against Kevin's restraint. I waved and signaled and shouted ... or was there suddenly no voice and then a wind and then them reaching where the wolf had turned in, into the trees?

It took all night, sitting outside in those chairs, for me to ask myself: *why wasn't I afraid?* Sure, I had been shooting a good long while late that afternoon, in the lovely lighting of the sunset, focusing on greens of mosses and tans of mushrooms. This had relaxed me. And then I had been following a deer trail across a carpet of pine needles, pretending, childlike. But even so?

I looked at those seven photos on my computer screen at high resolution and zoomed in. And on the sister monitor brought up, next to them, images of DEC-confirmed wolves. There is no doubt.

I have no doubt. Tell it to the wolf that he isn't supposed to be here and get on home au nord de Canada before ICE grabs you ahead of ENCON on their way up 81.

Maybe k.d. lang will meet you at the border and sing a song of you. I shot her, once, too. Up close and very personal, as I cried and I cried as she sang, "Hallelujah." Can you believe me when I tell you I have those photos, too?

A lot of time has passed as I sit here. Framing and reframing what I knew, thought I knew, didn't know. In the way I have wondered, I wonder whether two friends who knew Bill and worked in his wake knew what was happening, when, and how much.

Mostly, I wonder about Bill's lawyer (unnamed by the press), reportedly (as of today's news) getting a text about Bill's plan and calling the police, who arrived just in time to see his head explode.

If you work as a lawyer with clients under pressure, you are going to get that call. Your client is dead. Your client has their spouse hostage and is threatening to kill her. Your client is stalking the judge and stands across the street from where he and another judge take lunch together every Friday.

You will reach for the receiver. You will break any code of silence. And then you will live and you will lawyer and: You. Will. Go. On. Because that's what the job demands.

Your only salvation will be that no one cares about who is the lawyer. You and your pain will remain anonymous.

Dog Bite

Our dog bites me in the face. In a split second, the open, snarling jaw of an eighty-pound Redbone Coonhound clamps down across my face. I feel and smell the exhale of his breath on the exertion. I think *he missed me by the amount of space I put between us as I pulled back in slow motion in that weird way that time bends when something really bad is happening.*

But then it snaps back to real time as my forehead goes warm with the rush of blood that goes through the fingers of my rising hand. It splashes deep, healthy red onto hardwood floors.

"Kevin, I'm bleeding—a lot," I say to Kevin, who's on the far side of Red.

"Red." He came with that name, but I'm not convinced he knew it when we drove him away from the shelter last month. He's learned it in the meantime, though. When we say "Red," he looks, he comes, he knows it's time for breakfast and dinner.

A Redbone is an overgrown Dachshund. Chestnut in color. Broad of ears. Exceptional of shape. Not to be confused with the Rhodesian Ridgeback. Red's smarter than any dog I've ever met.

Maybe the problem is that I have raised Labs, one male, one female, both rescues. The latter got juggled from one house to the next until me and a former husband and a forever stepson split apart.

That breed is retriever, to fetch the dead duck of the hunter, where to break the skin of the bird is a "bad boy." Labs love their people.

What did we know? We were impressed after the fact to learn Redbones have been bred to fight bear, wolf, and raccoon. There are at least two gangs of coyotes on our mountain and its valleys, and that will come in handy. Just in case.

But we don't know his life journey on the estimated five years before the four shelter months after he was picked up with a Rottweiler as a couple of strays. Did we get enough eye contact? Did we spend enough time with him before we said yes? As he pulled on the leash and he dazzled us with his beauty, were we falling in love without thinking?

Kevin helps me to the kitchen, to a stainless steel sink that will easily clean. And now a fresh towel. Soaked in cold water. I ask for a bag of ice. Kevin slides the chair and guides me to sit down.

"No," I say, "the Ziploc isn't in the drawer with the Cling Wrap and all the aluminum foil; it's in the cupboard all the way over there on the left." *Doesn't that make sense in case of an emergency?*

I'm aware of a big, red dog, moving stealthily among us, in the kitchen, and I actually wonder, *Is he done with me?*

No, he's not. He's licking up my blood from off the floor. My hearing has skyrocketed through two ears, flooded with adrenaline. The smell of my own blood starts to gag me.

I am unyielding in my application of pressure to my face. My eyes are safe and I can see, even though now they are covered by the towel and the ice and my hands, both of them, as I start to slide toward the counter for fuller support.

God, don't let me faint. Don't make me sick. Stay focused. Stay in control. What next?

Kevin starts to worry about shock because my legs start to jiggle. For me, that's normal. But it's the first time he's seen it. It rarely ever shows, externally, unless you know exactly what to look for, and this jiggly leg thing, in first one leg, and then in both, is the certain onset of shock and hypoarousal. It will be three to four hours before my brain will be able to start clearing all the chemicals it's now releasing to numb me down, slow me down, keep me alive as "flight" becomes an inward journey.

Kevin calls 911. I'm going to have to fight to speak clearly so that the police and the EMTs will be able to understand me.

When I have an attack, my speech tends to slur like a drunkard. The chemicals at the back of my tongue inhibit movement, pooling instead inside my ears and amping up the volume. My eyes droop. My gaze droops with it. My eyes are closed right now, anyway. I don't want to see. It's a horror film, and if I look and if I imprint these images of the dog and of the blood, it will make it exponentially harder to someday get over this.

Kevin is quiet and calm and takes the leash and takes the dog outside to his big, new kennel. It's so new, it's still wearing its price tag: $299 from Country Max. Unbelievably, even though we haven't gotten this far in his training for him to even be in the kennel in the dark, let alone by himself in the kennel in the dark, Red says nothing.

It's added up quickly, hasn't it? The kennel for the farm. The kennel for the Webster house. The travel kennel for the truck. Heartworm, flea and tick shampoo, bowls. More than one thousand dollars already invested. The initial ROI was fabulous. Investors will now be shaken by the unexpected decline in returns.

Sorrow courses through me. Guilt and sorrow. I may have cost this dog his life.

Let sleeping dogs lie.

Now I know why.

I was only crouching down to pet him, to let him know we were on our way upstairs to bed, in case he woke later and was confused and got stressed out.

Where is Maggie? Oh, God, what I wouldn't give for my girl Maggie! My yellow Lab girlfriend with whom I was inseparable when the two of us were on our own. Peter took her away from me. He kept the house on the lake. Eventually, he stopped sharing Maggie, stopped returning my calls, left me with her purple, nylon collar and leash hanging on my doorknob because he wanted her in leather and so didn't care if those were left with me.

That was last year.

Little by little, I vacuumed up the last of her hair. From the living room. From the car interior. From my clothes. I gave up eventually and washed her quilt. Sadness forced me to pick up and pack up her bowls. My girl who would never have turned on me.

Is it a one bite rule?

How could I think that a growl was a snore?

Why was I so stupidly confident to crouch, extend my hand, and let that pull my body and face so close to our sleeping dog?

I need love too badly for my own good.

Kennel Talk

Red is outside. I am inside. I am at the kitchen window, looking out at a traumatized dog.

We've run a range of conclusions, emotions, and shock since Monday night. If this had happened to the little girl who lives next door, whom we love ... If it had been a mere quarter inch to the right or to the left and I had lost eyesight ...

What we don't say is the truth: "What if he had made full contact and ripped off your face?"

Instead, we play and replay our gratitude that having done yoga and having done gardening in Garland Pose, I had both the reflex and the balance to pull back. I can still feel the pressure rolling under my feet, front of the ball to the back of the ball, my toes exerting pressure as I rocked the span of perhaps three-quarters of an inch.

It's why haircutters say, "Are you sure? Because this is an inch," as they gesture before starting to cut.

Kevin is upset. At Red for biting me. At me for not being angry at Red.

But you see, Kevin, this is what will tell you how much I have already been victimized. My parents raised me to love the hand that struck me. Taught me that was Christian. Explained to me this is how it was in any other house on the street where we lived.

15

I am fighting so hard to be the woman I want to be: unafraid of aggression, capable of facing an aggressor, deliberate in my response.

If society says parents the world over can hit their children as part of a good upbringing … If those parents have no accountability and most certainly are not euthanized … Should Red meet that ultimate fate because he unpredictably took one bite at a face that had already been hit?

It's the most difficult analysis I have ever conducted. Not to react. Not to take an easy out that this situation would provide. To do what I was taught: to just walk out there and carry on, as if nothing had ever happened.

But it did.

And my face looks so ugly that I can't truly know. What will Red think when he gets a good look at me?

Kevin has gone out, for a moment, to a doctor's appointment, and it's about time for Red's dinner. He's seen me, here and there for a moment in our completely inverted routine. We had been inseparable, training our day-long priority for nearly a month. Now, he was up, fed, out to the kennel by Kevin, walked by Kevin, dinner by Kevin, inside for bedtime by Kevin. Only thus far Tuesday and half a day Wednesday, but I was drowning in internal conflict all the same.

Me, the woman who just saw a wolf, is now haunted by the image and the feeling of the jaws and the breath of a Coon. Now I sleep with a light on and Monday night left on a movie all night long. "Hope Floats." Sleeping. Waking. Tearful. Hearing Red right on time at 6:25 a.m., Kevin getting straight out of bed to go feed him and walk him, saying, "You stay here, until he's out."

When I was in high school, I called a boy—once. I asked him if I could stay at his house that night. It was just about graduation time. A pile of us had gone as friends to the prom and down to the Jersey shore the next day.

I forgot my house key. So, in this pile full of sunburned teenagers, we stopped at an aunt and uncle's house, where my parents were to be for a barbeque, in order that I might retrieve a house key.

I don't really know why I did it that way. I had broken into the house how many times just by popping my bedroom window screen.

In my memory there is only about fifteen seconds and two scenes left of what had been a full-length Indie that simply fades and fades as I no longer have use to keep it with me. It's down to the groan in my voice as Dad says the key is with the next-door neighbor, and his hand coming into the car to hit me in the face. The next shot is the silence of no words from anyone as we drive, staring forward, to my house.

Michael, who was driving, who was my friend and my prom date—he was the first. The first to commit suicide a year and not much more later. I remember parents who were kind, their new puppy in the kitchen (*Stay on the linoleum!*), Dungeons and Dragons on Friday nights to which I drove myself in that 1972 Dodge Dart.

But his parents sent him to The Citadel Military College of South Carolina, and that was the end of it all.

It couldn't have been too much later that evening, I made this phone call. I've no idea why or where possibly could such an idea ever have taken flight. The sun was still somewhere, though low and to the west. My body hot with the day's sun. My face some combination of red from the burn and the slap. I dialed the number, handwritten on a scrap of ripped paper, to reach out to a boy I met that very day, as one of the kids who went to and knew Michael at his high school. A long hold after I said I truly can't ever seem to remember what. The boy's voice returning to the phone to deliver the message that his parents thought it would be better for me to stay at home and work it out with my parents.

Me, taking down every award ever received, packing every trophy ever won. And nothing, not one word never-upon-ever being said about two, big boxes then in my closet wearing the words "Awards" and "Stay Out."

My mother's eyes—when?—scanning my room, briefly, realizing, clenching her jaw. We had a different kind of one-on-one fight as I reached that senior year. Never defended me in front of my father. Stopped striking me on her own, left the assault at all verbal, and kept it in that mode all the way to her end.

So I mix dinner the way Red likes it, and out I go. I talk my way to him, as soon as I turn the corner around the house and walk into his line of sight. He looks. He looks and isn't sure, but I have food. I'm not sure either. My tone's not quite normal. My gaze is too straight.

So here I am and now he sees me and Red looks down.

He knows. All that needs be said has just transpired.

I go to the door of the kennel and Red backs up. He seems to cower. My heart? It simply breaks. I start to cry but can't let myself do that; never show fear to a dog.

I put his bowl down, wait patiently for him to eat, while I start to tremble and do emergency reaction planning. I don't believe in moving about during my dogs' meals. They should relax. Be able to enjoy. A reward for their day. My pleasure to serve them. But I've closed the gate behind me, to keep Red in, and it keeps me there, too, with Red in a small space.

Red's done eating. He backs away from his bowl. I back my way out of the kennel. Signal Red to stay, but he's already backed up, trying too hard to show me he's mastered what Kevin has taught him in less than two days. *See, Mom, you can trust me.* I go to the outside. Crouch down eye level to Red.

At first, Red comes over slowly, and examines my full face. He looks at me more deeply than I have dared to look at myself. I can't look. The stitches, dried blood, swelling, bruising under both of my eyes. What I have seen, I consider to be a blessing, don't need to make a study of it or make it harder upon myself.

I close my eyes. Let him look as long as he wants. Hear him sniff a single sniff.

And then he leaves me. Walks away. Walks over to the far corner and dissociates himself by staring off into the distance. Sits slowly. Sits dejectedly. Sits as if he's holding back tears, and that moving too quickly will cause them to spill.

I sit, too. Awkwardly plop down on the spot. Sit with Red, whom already I love. Remember everything that is beautiful, already packed into these thirty days. How he circles and circles and paws and does more circles before he lies down to go to sleep. How he loves it when the blanket falls off of the bed and onto him, just his toes hanging out for us to see. How he finally—*finally!*—started trotting and cantering and loosening his limbs this past Sunday at the farm. How cheered and proud we were of him!

Kevin and I have been healing each other for now more than a year, and we have love and we have skills to share with Red.

Red bit me in the face.

What do I do with that fact?

I am no longer a child. This decision is now ours to make.

He Speaks with Confidence

An appellate brief is due. I don't want an extension. I want a diversion. Work will do me good.

It was like this, growing up. Want to stop your parents from fighting? Win a prize. Stop the hurting? Good report. Get time off? Make the newspaper.

Homework. Work-work. Best place to run and hide. Purpose. Need. "Too busy now to talk Mom. I have to get to court."

But this time, Red is hurting and I am hurting and it isn't going to work to duck and cover. I can't even sit at my desk. There's no line of sight to Red, except through the kitchen and plant room windows, and those aren't near my desk.

I go outside.

Outside with the draft Brief, the approved Record on Appeal, blue pen, red pen, highlighter, and a blanket.

Red wags, slowly. Wag-wag. Pause. Wag-wag ... wag? Steals a look, but doesn't look. Doesn't know what I'm up to at this midday hour, but isn't going to let curiosity overcome _____? (I'm still not clear on what he's feeling. *Oh, Red.*)

I plop down. Day two.

He goes to the other side of the kennel, which means at his size, about two standing body lengths away.

I talk to him, patiently, about what I'm doing and why and that I thought I'd do it all outside with him.

I'm nervous. I have to admit I'm nervous. He's on the other side of a metal cage. It's not affixed to a cement platform; it rests on the grass. It's also high at six-foot-something, but not so high he couldn't scale it. Those seconds wouldn't put the kitchen door between me and him, if he chooses to pursue and attack me.

Crazy. I know. If I'm that afraid, why am I here? Why not go inside?

Why is this so important to me? Why can't I just decide what to do and call the county back and call the town back and tell them that the threat has been contained and eliminated? No one else will have to worry?

The sun is shining. I put my back to the sun. Wounds and healing and huge antibiotic pills broken in half, mercifully, by Kevin.

I am sideways to Red, who steals glances.

He woofles and coons at other dogs getting walked. We're far enough back from the road that no one pays mind to my face. A quick smile and a wave. None of the dogs say anything back to poor Red, who's making so much of an effort.

This is ridiculous.

I pick everything up and go to the other side of the cage. Plant myself next to Red, where he is sitting. He is surprised. He walks a circle around his cage, pausing in the back, diagonal corner. I get more direct, call him over. He comes. Sits. Lies down. Raises one eyebrow and peeks sideways at me.

Where did I learn all this taming of creatures? The story of *The Little Prince* and his rose? Some story I heard once about a fox? Did someone tame me?

It doesn't hold. It's inconsistent. He relaxes. He jumps up to bark at a dog. He works his way back, only to leave me, again.

But by the time Kevin gets home, Red is happy to see him, and then he's acting like it's the first time he's seen me and then the three of us go on a walk around our three-quarters of an acre suburban yard. Red found the reset button. He's decided to experience trust. Allow for the possibility that he's not going to be beaten. And each one of us forgets for a moment and we are a happy family.

This man, Kevin, lets me hold his hand too tightly, and not without trembling, as we walk away and Red starts barking, again, at yet another dog. (We live on the corner of the road that leads to a multi-acre public park.) Kevin doesn't understand all of what I'm doing or why I'm doing it. I wish he did; then he could tell me what we should do.

Instead, Kevin simply holds me.

He holds me together.

He listens as I hash and rehash and we wish for a list of different outcomes, but can't escape that it would have happened one day. We can only conclude: *better now and better only this much.*

Kevin lets me sleep with a light on in our bedroom, opens his arms, lets me lie in one specific position, clinging and pressing my body onto his, never complaining if the Neosporin smell upon my forehead is right below his nose. He never once says anything other than "It's healing beautifully, Babe" and "It's going to be fine, Buttercup." He speaks with a confidence that I need and that is true.

It's not our first crisis in only our first year and some months.

Tomorrow we must make our decision.

So much has been taken from each one of us as children, as a couple.

Where is the answer for Red that will provide the answer for us?

The Other Side of 4:00 a.m.

It has always been this way for me: I just need to know that it's the other side of 4:00 a.m. Whether it's a death, a bad dream, raw fear. After 4:00 a.m., I can tell myself, honestly, *It's the other side of night and nearly into sunrise.* That's all I need to stay calm, fall back to sleep, leave whatever haunts me in yesterday's dark.

I bear signs of having been a recent victim of serious violence. Dried blood and stitches on my face. And not just anywhere on my face, but between my eyes, across my brow, up my forehead. There is swelling. There are black eyes.

I am treated differently.

On primary Tuesday, I went out to vote. As I walked into the room, a woman I knew only a little said, "Tell me that isn't a dog bite." An entire room of people turned, in silence, to stare at me. How peculiar to think that a mutual friend tried to put us in touch with her for a Lab puppy at about the same time we discovered our Red.

Two men come to cut down six dead pines, hired by the town, discussed at some great length back in July. I hadn't gotten to taking out the forsythia bushes, four years old, grown from cuttings, from underneath the pines. If they're not taken out, they'll be trampled.

The men ask me nothing. Their manners are too good. Instead, they won't let me dig, take it over, shovels, buckets, and all. "Show me where?" "Is this one?" "Just move those weeds over, please." "Oh, I see it now."

They are swift.

I apologize and appreciate.

They remain too polite. They dig up thirteen forsythia bushes, each about two-feet-high. I have that many buckets. I'm a little shy on dirt.

After the doctor follow-up on Tuesday, we went to Starbucks. Kevin tells me on Wednesday how women shot him dirty looks. I'm appalled at their misjudgment.

I, too, had caught a couple of glances as we walked into the shop, so I had looked down, shrunk myself inward, took on the manners of a ghost.

And when my drink was served, I had babbled to Kevin, "Oh, I should have asked for chocolate flakes—you know they have them—that would have been over the top too much." I had managed a small smile, not wrinkling my forehead. It had taken some courage to make that small talk, to allow myself to turn that corner, to peek into the land of the living.

He had asked the barista, "Do you have chocolate sprinkles?" as I had spoken over him, "No, that's okay," believing they charged for them, as she said, "Yes," all too quickly and took haste to put them on. I had said, "Thank you," like a child, but her "You're welcome" was spoken to the counter before she turned her own face quickly back to the coffee machines.

We have an expectation people like me will stay at home. Or stay in cars. Or at least stay in the yard. Out of view, doing something productive.

You don't see people like me out in public or at a restaurant.

Unless there's "dynamic," and by that I really mean a strong, violent dynamic.

See, Kevin's right. The interpretation was proud aggressor on parade with his victim. Invading Starbucks. Intruding on daylight. Out in the open of the city's richest suburb. The worst of aggression in private is often the most public of displays of the unhealthy couple.

But we hold hands and we are in love, and how does one miss the million little cues that say "Hey! He's one of the good guys!" Holds the door. Touches the small of my back. Asks what I'd like and then orders. Gets it right. Gets me chocolate sprinkles.

They don't understand. This beautiful face? This once teenage beauty queen? Already scarred. For life. Through and through. Years of abuse. Thirty-two years of abuse. Could you see that when it was happening? The dog bite is what?! *by comparison.*

Only the rarest of person (twice) ever did notice and bother to ask me some questions.

For thirty-two years, no one I knew—and I mean no one I knew—called the police, talked to my parents, removed me from home, or filed for divorce on my behalf.

I was a goddamned family lawyer living and working with a time bomb of a first husband and no one helped. Saw. Reached out.

Only after I kicked it. Only after I broke free at age thirty-two did two women ask. One, Auntie Jen, who said they didn't know what to do, and really who did? The year 1976, a bicentennial year. Auntie Jen, Uncle Jack, Auntie Lily, on a trip here from the UK. In 1976, I was ten (10). The 1972 Dodge Dart taking us from Ho-Ho-Kus, New Jersey, to Washington, DC, and then back home.

Then Ann, my piano professor for the four years at Wheaton College. Oh, that was sweet. Four full years and a degree with heaps of honors from a women's college, surrounded by feminists, learning the philosophy of Betty Friedan, and I was invisible. Oh, yes, feed me on your fiction. Suffer only the poor inner-city mother on welfare, two black eyes, a child on each hip looking sad. Quietly pay your private college tuition for a degree from the New England Intelligencia. Please wear your pearls. It's not proper for a lady—

Crows squawk.

About what, exactly? Too much fuss.

Dappled predawn through a pine tree. Our second story. One huge loft. Cutting down the pine trees didn't change the lighting; too far over, perhaps downstairs will get more sun?

My eyes are swollen. My range of vision, narrowed.

Random, arrhythmic pain darts across the wound. Are my nerve endings talking and healing or faltering and shutting off?

SATURDAY, SEPTEMBER 17, 2016

Cortland County SPCA

You can know something is coming, but it can still grab you—hard. Grab you and choke you and send tears streaming down your face.

Having been raised by a heavy-handed British father, these kinds of things are supposed to be kept under control. Neatly locked away. Hidden from view, even among immediate family. "Stop crying!"

I was not that child. Or maybe I once was and then I wasn't.

In the photo albums, of which there are many, I am the only child. The star of the show. The little girl who in first grade at Ho-Ho-Kus Elementary School got in trouble with Mrs. Clay for drawing myself, in between my parents, when I was asked to draw a picture of my family.

Fear and aggression. It's the theme of the week. Did I get bitten because Red was afraid, or did his fear only come after, as he cowered, without any reason from us, because he learned the feel of a beating from someone else? And what of Bill? A fear, then, too, that was too great? That made him hurt himself? And his family. And his friends.

If there is any blame to be had, it is the individual who taught Red so much fear that he was conditioned to try to defend himself. It is Red who is the victim, and it is Red who may have to pay the ultimate price.

By Saturday at noon, he is surrendered to Cortland SPCA. We drive three hours one way. The day is beautiful. Past lower Sodus Bay where we have stopped and he has swum. Down yet another route between a Finger Lake, past an independent coffee shop with a couple and a large dog in a harness, sitting casually outside.

We go slowly and Kevin is driving and Red is in his travel kennel in a truck bed that's filled with those forsythia bushes. Dug up in haste. Somehow surviving in their plastic pots. Windblown and roadway battered and losing most of their leaves. Red is unfazed by the spectacle.

Seven black kittens greet us in the waiting area as we arrive, leaving Red in his crate on the truck. We're loaded, arms full of food, of toys, of heartworm and flea and tick repellants, and it's as if we're porters for Red the Magnificent, headed off to the wiles for a bear hunt.

Leah reassured us on the phone. Red will not be euthanized; he will be worked with, by professionals, after being tested for triggers.

"Triggers." It's a whole new vocabulary. Baby dolls and crying dolls and food aggression.

On the drive down, I write out four pages of notes about Red. All his nicknames. How to mix his food the way he likes it. That he's too afraid to go up staircases; they literally make him whine and retreat.

I am honest. I describe his bite as "vicious."

That's the thing about violence that really gets the victims: the speed and the randomness. That's how I define "vicious." You're living by the rules that aren't written. The whole thing goes rolling along. And then the "BAM!" like a grenade, an IED. One split second of awareness and then you take the impact.

We wait there at the counter, me, my eyes downcast, my arms full of Red's stuff. Leah appears, and it's a blur. I'm talking. She's reading my notes. I'm asking for a copy. Kevin goes to get Red. And when he gets in there, strangers ooh and aah, and Red goes off with a volunteer, away from us, behind a closed door, without even one look up or one look back.

I lose my mind. All the anger at whoever treated him badly. All the injustice in my own life. All the words for every other victim I've represented, as a professional, for whom I have been even-keeled.

The tears just flow. In public. And I don't even bother to wipe them away.

Kevin leaves. I know that he cries, too. And so I exit because where we need now to be is within us, together.

I'll cry about this more than once and for more than just one more day. I'll call in once, more confused when they tell me they tried some testing but can't do sleep testing because no one is there at night. And then I won't call back. And then little by little, I'll stop liking shelters on Facebook and I'll stop petting dogs in the park, and I'll just go on wishing for a yellow Lab girl puppy. I never had a puppy. Maybe then ... But even then ... Now I know. I know.

Heal Each Other

It's the day of Bridget's wedding. I think about all the ordained men and women who have stroked their thumb upon my forehead to make the sign of the cross.

"And they will know you by …" said the voice I heard in those moments of shock after the bite when looking at my blood upon the floor. That voice I have heard before, once, twice? No, a few times. It rises from deeper within than the dimensions of the human body. There are no words to explain or express the experience of traversing from the human to the divine.

And so on this Sunday morning, after the climax of our love, is it any wonder that as I reach up to stroke Kevin's brow as he looks down upon me that the meaning of these words should come forward to be conscious?

I will forever bear the visible marking of the cross. There in the same lines and spacing as if the priests and the bishops and the fathers across my life had etched it in, one stroke by one stroke, until it at once became visible.

How will I kneel to take another communion?

Now the priest and all the world will be able to see it, the difference between this scar and all the others.

Everyone I hold dear bears scar upon scar.

Is it fortunate they don't all show, or would it be helpful, if we could see them? If Red had been marked, would we have passed him by? Our Maggie bore scars we could see, yet we adopted her. Our Theakston attacked vacuum cleaners, brooms, and rakes, with a bark to wake the dead and a focus borne of bad things. But we kept him.

And maybe that is the cause of much sorrow—that we don't know and understand and give respect to what's come before. We simply persist. Start anew. Run away from. Move ourselves on to what's next.

We stop at funerals, as a few of us did last Friday. For a moment, we ask hard questions, saying, "Bill (a different Bill), would you have thought Bill to be at risk to commit suicide?" And Bill says, "No," but adds some thoughts, and the four of us then give silent pause.

Red's tag is in between us on the table now as we drink our morning coffee in the trailer on our mountain. The tag is pink! But Kevin was right; it was the color to stand out against his fur. It says "RED SISSON," two phone numbers, and then "REWARD!"

And it is the truth! It is the truth. Hundreds and hundreds of dollars later, it's still the truth. Past kennels and vet fees, past dog bowls and travel crates. I would pay a fortune to lift away Red's past, so that his true essence could be with us. So that he could be here on this morning up on this mountain. Our dog we so love, in spite of what's happened.

It's the love Kevin and I give to each other. We're both so scarred that it's amazing he is this handsome and he thinks I am beautiful.

One day, a year and a half ago, barely knowing each other, just one date over coffee of nearly three hours, we stood upon the sidewalk in a small town near where he grew up. Kevin, suddenly sharing words I don't remember precisely about the events that changed the course of his very life when he was just a young man.

How I cried, moments later. I stopped the truck just down the road. I had to; I couldn't drive. The sky exploded into a fire I'd never seen before, but took it then as a sign, accepted it as The Word of the Beloved Holy Mother.

I photographed that sky, so I will never forget.

Three years earlier, I had considered going into a convent. Was simply finished with the life that I'd known, wanted refuge, wanted solace, wanted to be part of a greater devotion. I had no idea where else to turn.

I selected France, which I've loved all along, and where I knew such places continued to exist.

I started making decisions about selling and donating it all, except perhaps for my writing, my photography, my books, and my piano. Made a very long list for disposition. Sent it to the lawyer as part of finally making a Will.

Took my wedding ring to the jeweler and asked him to inscribe "Holy Mother" on its inside.

For three days I cried, having finally taken off the ring blessed by the priest, who had wrapped our hands, even as I married an athe-ist. He was divorcing me. Nothing had been true, if ever it was. And he and the more than 400 stitches covering his body asked me to go away and not return. His love, it seemed, was over, even though I had loved him more than he, it seemed, was capable of loving himself. A second divorce.

It was not to be—the convent. God wanted me on the battle-field. The sky blew up. A sunset turned into flames. And I was given the sign I had offered up to God when I had asked for the remainder of my life to be spent in sanctuary.

"If you still need me, you're going to have to give me a sign I can see. I am otherwise seeking peace."

I've been afraid of big dogs my whole life. *Who knows why,* I'd repeatedly say. And yet, we fell in love with and we adopted our Red.

I wasn't afraid of Red. Didn't even see him as a "big dog," nei-ther Rottie nor Dobe nor Pit nor German Shepherd.

But as I confronted my fear, I viewed his teeth, through metal kennel walls, and they were huge. And when we walked him, a day or two ago, and he treed a squirrel, he stretched upward along the trunk of the walnut tree, and he was far taller than all 5'4" of me.

I guess scars haven't served me as much of a warning. I never learn. At nearly fifty, I still believe that love can do it, at least one-on-one love. Arm the borders, have rigorous immigration policy, but heal each other.

Trust

I look out in the yard. The kennel is gone. Kevin is off returning it. He was thoughtful to call ahead to the store. I reprinted the charge slip. I should have helped him, but I couldn't.

Both of Red's beds are now under the piano. I brought the smaller one over, right away, as if Red could settle into it from afar. The Tupperware he took under it on his last night here is still there. I must admit, I was too shaky to stay with him while he had that extra half can treat, all mashed up along the sides—our newest game. It took him a happy, little while to eat.

How could this big oof of a dog have known that the space of my grand piano is the most sacred of space? He turned it into his doghouse from the minute he arrived at this house! Red had me bend every known rule on this planet. "Don't touch!" "It's not a table!" "Go wash your hands!" Between two dogs, one stepson named Sam, assorted friends, the occasional obnoxious adult. I have guarded this thing since I was sixteen-years-old.

I played the piano more for Red than I have for anyone in a good, long while. He didn't mind it. Didn't howl. Didn't roll his eyes. Didn't necessarily listen, moving from the bed down underneath it to the one just off the kitchen. (Red could hear.)

What do you say to a creature seeking sanctuary? To this living, breathing animal you have invited into your home?

Kevin speaks only the truth to me: that we tried our best and that we did right by Red and by us.

How do I tell anyone that yet again it feels to me as if I'm prohibited from having children? That the moments Red opened up were the same moments I let Hope enter in?

What is it they say? First get the dog, then get the baby?

There had been words. We had asked questions. We had said the word "adoption." We were talking already about children, trapped in foster care.

This has been a year so full of challenges. A heart attack for Kevin, age fifty-three. Two miscarriages and an end to the possibility of the longest of long shots. The death of two friends. The collapse of an employer. Selling off my parents' house and moving Dad into a home.

Would anyone dare to spit and blame us, if we both wandered off to France? Took a little cottage, over there in those mountains, walked evening and morn to hear vespers and engage in prayer? Just sat and talked and had a cup of coffee and held each other on a small, stiff, and uncomfortable bed at night as we wrote home, "Please send decent sheets!"

So much has changed of me since I was thrust out of my marriage. My mother's "spot"—a "little cancer"—that quickly killed her off. I've hit such highs in my fight for Lady Justice. Finally got some words before the United States Supreme Court.

I still looked young then: forty-five, but looked like thirty. At thirty-two, I'd looked like "college" and hoped it would last. Kevin has the same genes. Even as a father, the child upon his lap looked more like a nephew, for he couldn't be that old. Now I look old, maybe older than my age.

I don't know, really, how to feel about it all. This life the Lord calls on me to live. I know I have to trust, but what is that?

In just a week, I will turn fifty. Maybe this is all just related to only that. A midlife crisis, a misalignment of my stars, an early onset of something medical, the justification for a cruise around the world.

I won't be graceful about this juncture. I will live and I will become one of those fabled women of inner power. Those Annie Leibovitz–portraited women. Lips resting gently together. Body cloaked in the crowned jewels, fur collars, velvet robes, the orb and the scepter in hand. The naked, gray hair parted down the middle, kinky and untamed and lying upon a skin so soft that even the shoulders bear wrinkles.

It's all in the eyes with those women. The Queen of England upon her coronation day. Glenn Close and Meryl Streep and Susan Sarandon. They have always been women out front through the whole of my lifetime. Never girls. Never minimized. Not Goldie Hawn or Diane Keaton in their actual person or the roles that they played on world stages.

Free women.

Women who defied.

Women whose exuberance for life to be lived large could allow them to overcome, to transcend, to be the very shelter that they offer.

Angelina Jolie. Lara something or other superhero. Who found herself when she became an honorary ambassador for the UN. Lady Diana, whose photograph I clipped with a straight hand just days before her death, at an orphanage on the African continent, holding a girl so weak her head could not be supported by her neck.

In this effort, I have failed. I have failed Red in the sense that we may have given him the knowledge that not all mistakes are greeted with violence, but we did let him go to an uncertain future and he was already part of our family. We will both have to live with this, this man Kevin and I. Allow that maybe this is what was needed and maybe we didn't fail him. Hope that our time together was a meaningful contribution toward the healing of our Redbone named Red.

And go on.

Life is like this and it will be like this, again. Friends and family are going to die, and it will be sometimes unresolved. Wild creatures are going to come near us, who we will love and want to hold and to keep safe but instead must let go without a knowing of where that will lead them.

And those times will require a superhuman strength that has to be found and be nurtured and be grown.

If we can find that—if we can harness that—then there is a chance, however small. There is a chance that we will live. Take flight and live the life that God has given us. Know something of the Divine while we are walking here on Earth.

And maybe, just maybe, those transcendental moments will get us through the rest.

Nearly fifty years down.

Another fifty to go.

The women in my family have a tendency to live a very long life.

About the Author

Photo credit: Thomas Flint, photographer

Paloma A. Capanna writes because words are as necessary to life as air and water. A civil rights lawyer by profession, in her personal writing, she frees herself and her readers from the rules that would otherwise inhibit the sharing of words as we actually experience them. She lives in Upstate New York. This is her first published manuscript.

CPSIA information can be obtained
at www.ICGtesting.com
Printed in the USA
BVHW03*0314151018
529641BV00001B/2/P

9 781642 983814